How to Use This Book

These drawings are taken from the illustrations in my book The Invisible Lion. They are presented here in an accessible format for you to share with friends, family or clients. They can be used to revise the concepts, discuss the ideas raised or as a teaching aid for psychoeducation.

Each drawing is accompanied by a short explanation of the idea it illustrates. If you want more information on each then I recommend reviewing the blog at theinvisiblelion.com or reading the original book itself.

My drawings are intentionally amateur. I want everyone to feel like they can draw them for themselves to show the power of these ideas to others, or even to understand their own lives. I hope you enjoy this flipbook and it becomes a trusted friend on your journey to find, and to begin to pacify, your own invisible lions.

The Divided Brain

Our brains are divided into three parts; the human brain, the mammal brain, and the reptile brain. These layers of the brain have built up over the course of our evolution. Roughly speaking the reptile is responsible for the freeze response, the mammal is in charge of fight or flight, and the human runs our social engagement system.

Evolved Responses to Threat

This diagram represents the gears in our response to threat, which we cycle through, in reverse evolutionary order, in response to increasing the threat. Social engagement is at the top of the ladder, where we make friends to avoid threat. When this fails, we become vigilant to increase our awareness of threat in the environment. When the threat is real, immediate and all else has failed, we fight or flight. Finally, when that doesn't work, we freeze.

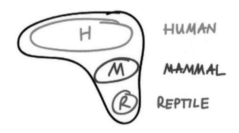

HUMAN

MAMMAL

REPTILE

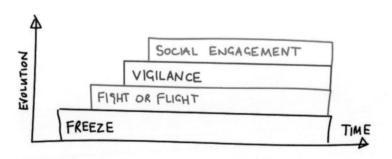

The Threat Response Cycle

The horizontal line in this graph represents time, and the vertical line represents the activation of our sympathetic nervous system (the one we use to respond to threat). When threatened, our activation goes up (or gets charged) and then returns to normal (homeostasis) once the threat has passed.

Charge in the Threat Response

At its resting state, the nervous system is not activated (or charged) to respond to threat. Once there is a threat, activation happens, and the nervous system is charged. Once the threat has passed, our activation goes down and the energy from the response is discharged, bringing it back to square one.

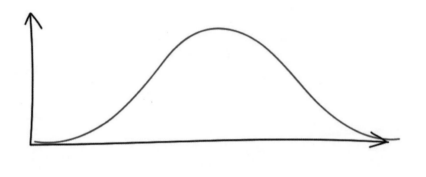

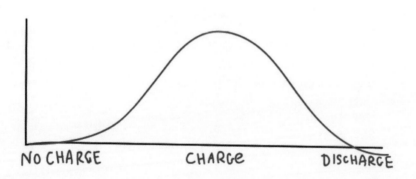

NO CHARGE   CHARGE   DISCHARGE

Overwhelm in the Threat Response

When the body is overwhelmed by its own response to a threat, it hits a sort of redline that it simply cannot go beyond. This is a problem because the threat is still there but the part of this graph above the redline is no longer possible to get to.

Freeze in the Threat Response

When a threat is overwhelming and our activation tips over this redline, we need to take a break. Our threat response freezes, and then when it is safe again, it all starts up in exactly the same place, carrying on as it would have if it had not stopped at all.

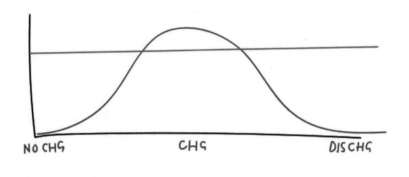

NO CHG   CHG   DIS CHG

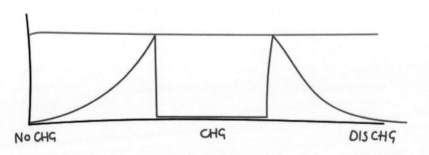

NO CHG   CHG   DIS CHG

6

Stored Activation in the Threat Response

The blue circles in the diagram above represent the frozen activation in response to a threat. We look like we are not activated, because we are not doing anything, but this is like a car which is not moving, even though its brake and accelerator are both fully pressed. The blue blobs represent this potential energy, the surge in activation which will happen when the brake is lifted. Once we feel safe again, this is what happens and then we discharge the stored energy.

The Story of the Lion and the Gazelle

From left to right, we have; a gazelle at the watering hole with a relaxed nervous system; a lion arrives and the gazelle is activated into fight or flight; the lion catches the gazelle and is about to eat it, so the gazelle goes over the redline and freezes; the lion is distracted from his kill and so the gazelle survives, which triggers the discharge of its stored up activation; the gazelle returns to rest and goes back to the watering hole. The discharge can be over in a minute or two and the gazelle's nervous system returns to rest (homeostasis) as if nothing has happened.

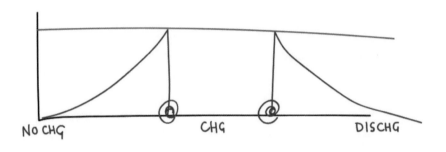

No CHG   CHG   DISCHG

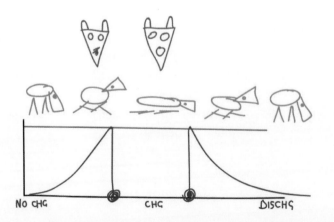

No CHG   CHG   DISCHG

Self Awareness

But what if the gazelle could see and analyse everything that is happening? Take each box in isolation and see how that would look to the gazelle. In Box 1 it is calm in a calm place; in box 2 it is running from a threat; in box 3 it is overwhelmed by being about to be eaten; in box 4 it is running from a threat, but there is no threat! If you add in self-awareness, then suddenly everything which had evolved to happen for millions of years doesn't make sense. And for a human, that's a problem; a threat even.

Dicharge Interupted

If you add in a new threat, just as the gazelle is trying to discharge the energy of the old threat, then the blue squiggly line, the charge, isn't fully released, or discharged. There has been no opportunity for it to get up over the redline and organically discharge back to its normal resting state. It can't get back to square one (homeostasis).

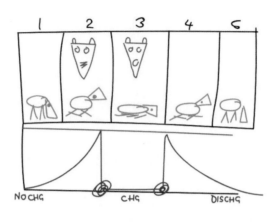

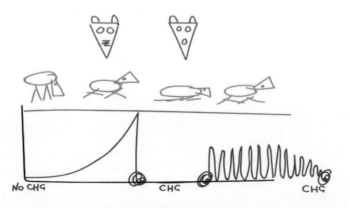

A Second Lion

Without getting back to square one (homeostasis), if a second lion appears, we will react more quickly and get more charged sooner than is ideal for dealing with the threat (the dotted line). We add into this second reaction the unfinished charge from our first threat, and that causes our charge, or blue line, to climb too quickly, reaching overwhelm before we've had a chance to have our optimal flight or fight response.

Third Lion, Fourth Lion, Hundredth Lion

When we don't finish responding to the first threat, and then the second threat, our response to every subsequent threat gets more and more dysfunctional. This is a viscous circle because we reach overwhelm more and more quickly, thus creating more and more charge to discharge later.

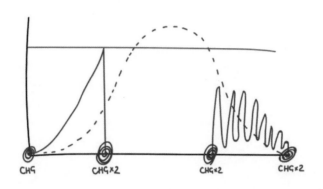

CHG   CHG×2   CHG×2   CHG×2

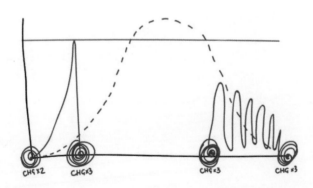

CHG×2   CHG×3   CHG×3   CHG×3

12

Dysregulation

After a while, our nervous system no longer works at all. It simply leaps around from high states of activation to overwhelmed freeze. This is the modern plague of anxiety and depression. Once our nervous system is dysregulated, we can no longer smoothly respond to any threat in the beautiful way that millions of years of evolution prepared us for. We have gone from a smooth analogue response to threat to an on-off digital response to threat.

Human Brain Filter

On the left is the ideal flow of reactions by the brains. The reptile and the mammal can react and the human brain allows a reaction to happen (you are reading this to make that possible!). On the right is what actually happens most of the time when we try to discharge energy to an earlier threat that we can no longer see; the human brain suppresses the organic reptile and mammal reactions.

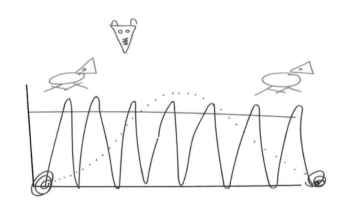

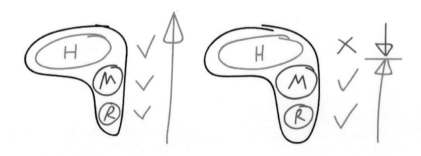

Distorted Reality

If the body feels like it is responding to a threat, but there in no threat to be seen, then it can be very tempting to "find" a threat on the outside. This plays havoc with modern life, in every area from our relationships to politics. We are in the habit of inventing imaginary lions to make sense of our bodies, and our human mind can be very convincing. The lion, however, is real; it is just in the past and therefore currently invisible, until you learn how to look properly.

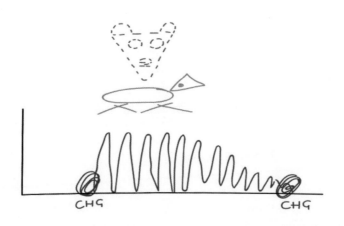

Baggage

When we are dysregulated, we collect a lot of unfinished responses to threat. This is called our baggage. The red squiggle above represents this baggage. Baggage is the accumulation of unfinished business that we carry in our nervous system. If you haven't finished dealing with a previous threat, it becomes baggage, and like the name suggests, you carry it around with you. Baggage can come from any adverse experiences which overwhelmed us and which we therefore have not yet finished reacting to.

A Trigger hits your Baggage

The green arrow in the diagram above represents a trigger. A trigger is anything that activates an earlier unfinished response to an earlier threat. Triggers are very personal and so different things trigger different people. If you were bitten by a dog when you were younger, for example, and didn't deal discharge your body's response to that fully when it happened, the experience may be stored in your body. If you hear a dog barking at a later stage, this might trigger you to go back to those unfinished responses, such as fear or flight, which might seem unnecessarily exaggerated responses to a third-party watching you and the dog.

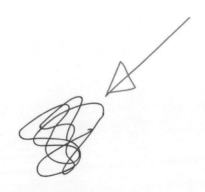

An Under Reaction

A response to a stimulus that is significantly less intense than the intensity of level of the stimulus itself. If I yell at you for something you didn't do, and you don't react at all, then you are likely to be under reacting. From the outside this person might seem completely calm. But inside, they are anything but calm. Usually they are clamped shut hiding all of their reactions because (and perhaps quite rightly) they are worried that they will explode.

An Over Reaction

The big red arrow represents your reaction to a trigger hitting your baggage. An over reaction is a response to a stimulus or trigger that is of greater intensity than the intensity of the stimulus itself. If someone tells me that a picture I drew is bad, and I scream at them for saying so as if my life is in danger, that is an example of an over-reaction.

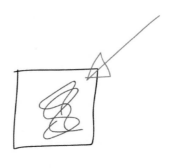

A Goldilocks Reaction

A response to a stimulus that is in proportion to the threat level of the stimulus itself is just right. It is the ideal reaction, instead of an over reaction or under reaction. In the fairy-tale of Goldilocks, she tested all the the beds, chairs and porridge of the three bears, with each being either too much, too little or just right. So, when your nervous system is not triggered, you don't have a reaction; you have a Goldilocks response, which is just right.

Three Reactions

So there are the three different types of reaction to a trigger. On the left, an under reaction. In the middle, an overreaction, and on the right, a just-right, or Goldilocks', reaction.

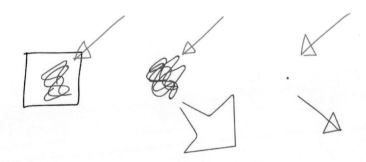

Boundaries

The blue shield represents a boundary around our baggage. This reduces the impact of a trigger, represented by the green arrow. So it might go down from a 3-out-of-10 to a 1-out-of-10.

Containment

This blue shield represents containment, which is how we manage our reactions to triggers (the red arrow). If our reaction without boundaries or containment was a 9-out-of-10, then, if we are really lucky, we can manage to get it down to a 3-out-of-10. We do this in part by reducing the intensity of the trigger (a boundary) to 1-out-of-10, and then by hanging onto some of our reactive energy (containment) thus getting a 6 reaction to a 3-out-of-10. This turns out to be perfect! A 3 for a 3, Goldilocks.

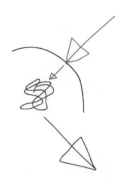

Full Circle

Here we see how the barriers of boundaries and containment create a circle. It becomes a whole shield around our nervous system creating boundaries to our triggers and containment to our reactions.

Internalising Boundaries and Containment

This holding for our nervous system is analogous to the way that a mother ideally holds her baby. The baby gets to grow up shielded and comforted, and slowly over time, this holding is internalised. Something magical happens and the dysregulation of an infant (not really baggage yet but looks the same) becomes held by the infant's own emerging strength. This is the benefit of a good childhood with a secure attachment. This is what it actually means.

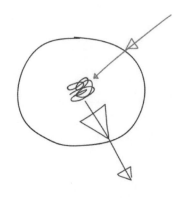

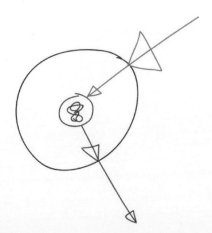

From Over Reactions to Just Right Reactions

When we practice boundaries and containment we move from the diagram on the left to the diagram on the right. We become a simulation of a Goldilocks reaction to all our triggers, looking to the outside world as if we have no baggage at all. This is a great start!

Soap Bubble

If we fail with either of our boundaries and containment, there is a knock-on reaction to the rest of us. The broken blue circle illustrates how the full shield is a bit like a soap bubble; one hole and the bubble pops, meaning that a failed boundary pops our containment and vice-versa.

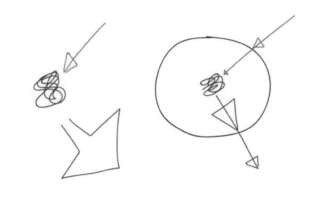

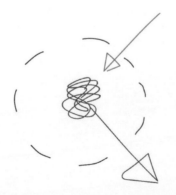

Over Reaction in Relationship with an Over Reaction

The triggers become bigger and bigger if we animate the diagram above.
One person's reaction becomes the next person's trigger.
These relationships are volatile and difficult to sustain.

Under Reaction in Relationship with an Under Reaction

There are little to no reactions in this relationship. The boxes around the baggage
represent the lack of a reaction, but instead internalisation. Such relationships often
become sterile and drift apart.

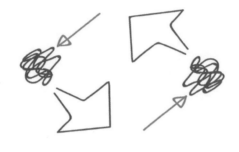

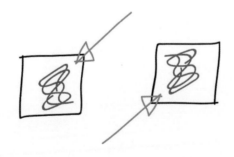

Over Reaction in Relationship with an Under Reaction

Above we can see that even an over reaction elicits little to no response from an under reactor. This can become an abusive relationship, especially if the lack of reaction triggers the over reactor. Sadly the lack of reaction from the under reactor means that they don't have the mobilisation to leave.

Goldilocks in Relationship with and Over Reaction

On the left is a well-regulated nervous system, and on the right is an over reactor, or dysregulated nervous system. This relationship is better for the over reactor, but wearing on the Goldilocks. It can be tolerated in short bursts.

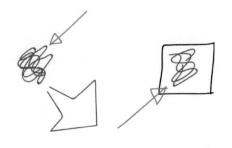

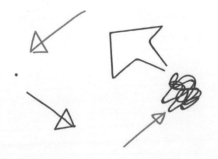

Goldilocks in Relationship with an Under Reactor

Above, we can see a well regulated nervous system with an under reactor. This will begin to wake up the under reactor, but might put the Goldilocks to sleep!

Goldilocks with Goldilocks

Two well regulated nervous systems working together.
This is pleasurable and sustainable.

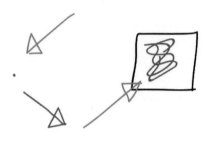

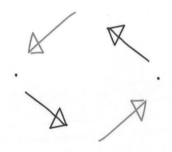

Healthy Simulation

The point of boundaries and containment is to fake this until you can make it. That's how dysregulated people learn to have functional, healthy and enjoyable relationships. Both nervous systems could be under or over reactors, but now have boundaries and containment to simulate well-regulated nervous systems.

Behavioural Recovery

To begin to restore our nervous system back to a place of regulation, we want to reach the diagram on the right from the one on the left. This allows us to begin to look like someone with no baggage.

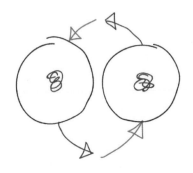

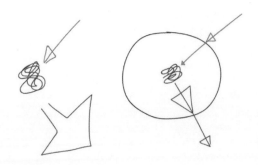

Discharge Recovery

Once our nervous system feel safe, we can practice getting back to our mammal brain and using it's automatic connection to our past to allow us to safely discharge the unfinished reactions to earlier threats from the baggage of our nervous systems.

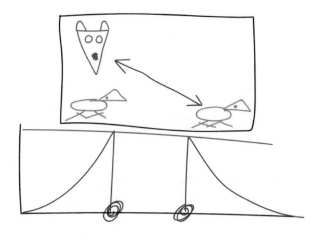

Further Resources

Visit www.theinvisiblelion.com to find out more about The Invisible Lion and the resources which go with it, including treatment ideas, further reading, related publications, videos and blogs.

About the Author

Benjamin is the Founder of NeuralSolution, Khiron Clinics and Get Stable. He is also an accredited psychotherapist and entrepreneur. He has had a rich and varied career, combining his interests in psychology, the media and business. In his twenties he founded two small businesses before starting a family, training as a psychotherapist and writing his first book which led to presenting a television series for the BBC.

More recently he has combined his business experience, clinical training and media skills to set up Khiron Clinics, residential and out-patient mental-health clinics, to lobby for more effective treatment in the public sector through his non-profit Get Stable, and to found NeuralSolution which delivers nervous system informed technology for behavioural health problems.

You can find out more about his life and his work at www.benjaminfry.co.uk.

Printed in the United Kingdom

www.theinvisiblelion.com

First Edition, October 2020

979-8693763081

Independently published

The
Invisible
Lion

The Flip Book

Created by Benjamin Fry